Author and Art:

"You express yourself well on these pages. I believe that your readers will be delighted to read what you have shared. I've not read poetry set up like this before and found it refreshing. I expect your readers will be looking for more from you in the days ahead."

-Terry Jacobs, Manuscript Review Specialist, Outskirts Press, Inc.

"There are times when an artist is able to speak to the reader on levels unknown. Randall is one of those authors. His works are an eclectic collection of works that will speak to your soul. As a professional who has produced many events in the genre of poetry, I've rarely come across such talent. Engaging in his works is something any reader should not miss."

-Maria Cavallaro, Ovations ENT Grp, Poetry Slam Talent Evaluator

"Extremely Talented Wordsmith. Scholarly with his Word-Play."

-Tony Watson, Rhema Records

"Wow, Congratulations Randall. We met about 10 years or so ago in a business capacity. I never imagined you were a talented writer. Your collection of Poetry and Children's writings are going to take the world by storm. Looking forward to your success!"

-Brent Boyd, BANA STUDIOS

"I am a librarian in Atlanta and I feel your work is Beautiful and Powerful. You are very talented and your work should be seen by the world."

-Cheryl Miller-Holmes, Librarian, Atlanta Public Schools

"I'm happy to inform you that you've been chosen to be on the cover of Black Authors Magazine! We're glad to welcome you to our June 2022 edition."

-Shanequa Campbell, Black Authors Magazine

Also by Randall Daniels

Poetry That Moves You

You Can BE, Who You Can SEE

For children

Great Britton (English & Spanish)

BOBO's Rhythm Rhymes 4 Youth

Books Written & Coming Soon

Toothbrush Tales

Poetry That Stirs

Edited by Evelyn L. Suesberry

"Simply, the most talented Author for whom I have edited."

A TRUE POETIC L♥VE AFFAiR

Everyone  Said Yes

UNTIL...

RANDALL DANIELS

Copyright © 2022 by Randall Daniels

All Rights Reserved.

No part of this book may be used or reproduced by any means, graphic, electronic, or mechanical, including photocopying, recording, taping, or by any information storage retrieval system without the written permission of the publisher-other than "fair use" in the case of brief quotations embodied in articles and reviews.

Paperback   ISBN 978-1-955798-14-3

As an Anti-Violence Activist
I Trademarked "BOBO The Champ"
Registered U.S. Serial Number: 90189418

Printed in the United States of America

This book is dedicated to my Baby Brother Jeffrey L. Daniels. For you MAN

Book design and all art work designed by Randall

Connect with me:

www.RandallDanielsBooks.com

& Follow Me:

Twitter: @Rdanielsbooks

Instagram: r.d.books

Facebook: Randall C Daniels

A TRUE POETIC LOVE AFFAIR

CONTENTS

INTRODUCTION OF JEFFREY AND BOBBI	3
DAY 2 The First Visit	9
DAY 3 The Unexpected Visit	19
DAY 4 Learning Each Other	33
DAY 5 The No-Show	39
DAY 6 Facing Reality	41
DAY 7 The Magical Day	49
DAY 8 Confused On What To Do	71
DAY 9 I'm ALL In	73
DAY 10 REMORSE	79
10 DAYS LATER	**89**
The Course of Four Lives Changed	
SCENES IN NEW YORK	**90**
5 Months Later A TRAGEDY	91
The Last Day Of The 5th Month	107
The 6th Month NO-SHOW	117
9 Months From The Moment They Met	123
3 Months Later Business in NYC	129
SEARCHING NYC	**134**
DISCOVERY SCENE	135
THE FINAL SCENE	146
ABOUT THE AUTHOR	**149**

CHARACTER VOICES & CHARACTER FONT

Bobbi's Voice: Times Roman

Jeffrey's Voice: Arial Bold

Narrative Voice: Harrington

Family's Voice: Baskerville

Hello there, how are you?

I'm well, thank you.

You have quite a beautiful smile, you're super sexy and, you're kinda cute.

Thank you Sir. You look quite debonair in your well-tailored suit.

I've been watching you, watching me,

Why did you take so long to finally speak?

Every time I looked up, you were with the same someone,

I figured he was your man, looks like you're having tons of fun!

Hmm, that's a good observation of you.

Is this something you routinely do?

Hit on someone new, to see where it may end,

Even though you're hugged up with your beautiful lady friend.

No, it's not what I routinely do. But It's something about You!

You caught my eye like Granny's pie that melts before I chew.

Ha ha very funny and you also have a smooth swag,

Plus, you have eye appeal that could get a lady in a snag.

Snags can be adventurous, could open a door,

But, it could also leave one's body, yearning for more?

Therefore, you'd better be careful, don't get yourself in trouble with your good thing,

You don't know the impact of what this girl will bring.

Blah blah blah, you think you got that love effect game?

Well, for the record, my claim to fame is quite the same.

Ok then, looks like we're both in a situation.

But I greatly appreciated your Charming Flirtation.

What are your thoughts on this wonderful Black-Tie celebration?

We come every year during Christmas and make a charitable love donation.

Nice! You have a good heart, you're kind of witty and kind of clever,

Please keep that delightful sense of humor, for EVER & EVER!

You too, I love your smile and your eyes,

So, saying good bye now, is probably most wise.

You have great conversation, and you're well put together too,

The heavenly creator of beauty, gave much love to you!

Boy bye! Talking with you was great,

But now is goodbye, I'm not trying to ruin your date.

Are you married?

Why? Are you married?

You can't answer my question with your question,

Bad etiquette 1-0-1.

Well, I did Professor, now what?

Don't make me break out the paddle, I'll spank that butt.

You're going to let your humor get you in trouble…

Naw, it'll be you looking for that daily double.

Oh! I see you got jokes,

Yes, what time is the curfew for you taken folks?

I beg your pardon, I don't have a curfew,

You're the puppyish one with ball and chain sitting next to your Boo.

She's hot and cute, hair is cleverly nappy and you look quite taken and look quite happy.

Like Christmas filled with toys from Pappy.

I must confess, your tuxedo has you looking like a Movie Star,

I'm sure you had to ask her permission to come over to this bar.

Oh No you Did-In!

You can see my ball and chain?

Well, you also look restrained like someone who's been caught, tamed and trained.

Your comebacks are crafty and you make me smile,

And I must admit, I haven't done a lot of that in a while.

Since you don't have a curfew, can I get to know the real you?

Just what are you asking me to do?

Come to my place where the air is fresher,

We can chat more and I promise you won't be under any kind of pressure.

The invitation is rather appealing and I would love to chat,

But I'm so sorry sweetheart, I don't know you like that.

I understand, you're afraid of me,

I'm not afraid of you, as far as I can see.

So please don't get it twisted, won't be no killing spree,

Just always know before you leap, this pretty face packs her heat!

Blah blah blah, here we go again,

Can I get a yes from my beautiful new friend?

NO. I'm sorry I don't know you like that,

But I'll let you stop by my Aunt's house to visit for a continued chat.

I'll call your bluff, while you're acting tough,

Are you for real or just talking stuff?

Here's my Aunt's address, not giving you my number,

So, stop by tomorrow before my body hits slumber.

Auntie's house stays full so I have no plans to cheat,

Just continued conversation with nothing to sneak.

Now, my name is Bobbi, what's your name?

My name is Jeffrey and will your Aunt be ok if I came?

Yes. I'll tell her there is a small possibility,

A charming fella may stop by that may have all of her tangibilities.

When the next day came around, Jeffrey was quite unsure of this step,

With a beautiful woman that loves him dearly, he has to consider any misstep.

Jeffrey, an entrepreneur, an inspiring author and poet trying to make his mark promoting his artwork.

Is engaged to Ashon Dupree an heiress with a billionaire net worth, who owns a majority stake in a television network.

Jeffrey's a charismatic ladies' man still sporting the golden physique of a boxer athlete.

Yet, quite a smooth romantic charmer, that many women want to meet.

Once a successful 3 sport athlete with potential fame and fortune ahead,

But 1 night of a brawl changed his world and left him hospitalized for 8 days instead.

Cut during the altercation that left him seriously close to losing that arm,

Jeffrey had no clue his sports life would collapse but he still had his smarts and his charm.

Still compelled to chat with Bobbi and enter her space,

But not quite sure of what's driving him, he did arrive to Auntie's place.

He was feeling a bit nervous which made him a bit shocked,

But there he was, glancing all around, before he walked to the door & knocked.

Hi, my name is Jeffrey, is Bobbi Here?

Yes.

Hello Ms. Bobbi, how are you?

Fabulous and you?

I'm great too and a little more comfortable not being in a suit.

Have I ever told you I like your swag, and that you're kinda cute?

No. You never told me, but I like the sound of that tho,

I must say you surprised me, I didn't expect you to show.

I told you my Aunt keeps a houseful because her cooking is lethal.

It's where I stay when I'm in town and catch up with my people.

Great home cooked meals, catch up on gossip and Auntie tries to cheer me with her jokes.

Always remember you have to keep an eye on her or she'll catch you in a hoax.

Oh, you're not from LA?

No, I live in New York, three thousand miles away.

What brings you to LA?

Christmas celebrating with my family and my fiancé.

How long do you plan to be in LA?

Only planning on a 10 day stay.

Where's your fiancé? Can I meet him?

He had to fly out this morning for some business prelims.

So that's who had you on lock down last night?

Based on last night, I'm kind of surprised he even lets you out of his sight.

Looked like lock down, click click!

Jokey jokes, please don't get me started with your beautiful picturesque chick.

By the way, does she know where you are?

Click click! Oh, and you looked quite nervous getting out of the car.

Girl, you need to stop with your lip service.

I have no reason to be nervous.

Everything is good, I was just in the neighborhood.

Hmm, hun this is Beechwood,

brothers don't just be in this neck of the woods.

Ok, you got me, this is a very upscale part of town.

Brothers could get arrested up here for just hanging around.

Can you go for a walk and enjoy some fresh air?

Sure, let me grab my shoes and my little boo Bare.

Ok, who is boo bear?

My French Bull Dog, her name is Bare.

She's been cooped up all day so she needs a little fresh air.

I thought boo bear meant a stroller and a baby,

No babies for me, although I've thought about it lately.

All good, hey little bear,

You look just like your mom, you two make a perfect pair.

Oh really. Now I look like a French bull dog, hahaha…

No, but she's gorgeously beautiful and quite unflawed,

Just like her mommy, worthy of my applause.

Nice bounce back, have I ever told you that you're kinda clever?

No, but I like the sound of it and you're welcome to say it whenever.

Do you like dogs?

Hell No! I Love Dogs!!

Breeding and raising German Shepherds use to be my side hustle

I was young and dumb back then with my hustle and bustle.

Hmm… What do you mean? That's a brilliant hustle as a teen.

But, in my world growing up, I raised a dominant queen,

We would breed her with the best males for pups muscular and lean.

Ok, but please don't tell me you're about to break my heart.

I hope not, but learning who we were and who we are now, is where we should start.

In my neighborhood you got recognition if you had a dog that could win a lot.

A dog that would win a lot at what hot shot?

Are you getting mad at me?

To be honest, I think we need to end this topic before I punch you in the eye and kick you in the knee.

You know youth can make some of the darndest choices sometimes,

And don't realize they are bad choices at that time.

Are you saying you didn't like it?

Didn't like what?

Fighting DOGS!

Do you want to hear the truth or do you want to hear what you want to hear?

I always prefer the truth my dear.

To be honest, I was a great trainer and I have always strived To Be Great At Everything I Do.

When you're growing up as a nobody, getting recognition from streets and your crew was cool.

At that stage in my life, I had no clue that dog fighting was cruel,

I would breed my beautiful Queen looking for her next beautiful jewel.

Some baggage and some background, I hope you don't hold against me.

Well, I have some baggage and some background that you surely don't see.

I could never be the one to judge another,

Live damaged by unforgiveness, just yearning for forgiveness from your very own mother.

In some of my youthful foolish ways, I lost a big brother.

So sorry to hear, if you choose to share, I'm a good listener and I'm all ears.

Nope, I won't share. It will put me in tears.

Everyone has a past with debts in arrears.

We're all fortunate that Christ paid our debts for us,

Although I'm a dog and animal lover your past wasn't totally treasonous.

Maybe don't say that too quickly, you don't know me yet.

I've already heard you from the inside, your heart, and I'll take that bet.

Oh, now you got super powers huh?

You are very Insightful and your personality appears to be quite fun.

What are the reasons you haven't smiled in a while?

You are a pretty cool guy and I like your style.

Thanks, but you didn't answer my question elusive one.

I know but that's a loaded question hun.

Oh wow! I graduated to hun?

Don't get the big head mister, I say that to everyone.

Yea, right! That slipped out because that's what you were feeling.

Some of your thoughts show on your face, you're not so good at concealing.

Boy bye! We've walked over 3 miles, are you tired yet?

Am I tired of you being evasive or am I tired from a little sweat?

Hmm, elusive and evasive, just what are you trying to say?

You already know the answer to that Bae,

Oh, I graduated to Bae?

Don't get the big head missy, I use that every day.

Yea, right! Good evening and thanks for the walk and your match play.

Boo Bare and I enjoyed your cleverness during our walk and talk today.

The pleasure was all mine,

I wish you much success in future quest & stay fine.

Thank you charming one, your smile really beams.

Go live the life of your dreams!

Bobbi's Aunt wasn't feeling well so Bobbi had concerns to some degree.

Auntie wasn't her usual self, vibrant and jubilee.

Jeffrey had a very successful morning meeting and was feeling brand new,

He decided to go see Bobbi, yet she didn't have a clue.

He was excited to share his excitement and zest,

And Bobbi, for whatever reason, he put her before the rest.

He drove to her Aunt's place with his heart in his throat,

Looking quite chic yet business casual in a stylish French sports coat.

Once again, he glanced all around before he began to knock.

And just like before, he became more nervous as the door began to unlock.

Hi, my name is Jeffrey, is Bobbi Here?

No.

For that very moment in time, Jeffrey stood there frozen.

In sharing his excitement, Bobbi was the person he had chosen.

He rode all the way to the boondocks because she hadn't given him her number.

And Bobbi not being there was quite a bummer.

Now he wasn't quite sure what he was doing,

But it was slightly apparent, a little something new was brewing.

She'll be back momentarily, would you like to come in and have a seat.

And by the way, I'm Bobbi's cousin and the name is Pete.

Thank you Pete, my name is Jeff.

Cool, my Mom is expecting Bobbi real soon herself.

Auntie I'm back and I have the things you needed.

I got the fruit you wanted and I found some unseeded.

I need you to feel better quickly, you're my favorite Aunt.

Thanks baby, I know I'm everyone's favorite Aunt and I'm putting you on record when I call my sister and I want to flaunt.

Please Auntie, you know I'm staying with Aunt Risha later this year.

So, let's keep our little secrets near and dear…

Jeffrey!! What the heck are you doing here?

I came to see you, share some news and share a cheer.

Jeffrey, you can't just pop up uninvited over here.

How will that look? Did you think about how that would appear?

My Aunt is sick and I look a hot mess.

I truly apologize and I didn't come to cause you any stress.

I stopped by to share a glimmering moment of my success.

Jeffrey I'm engaged so something like this could have turned out quite grim!

Baby I invited him.

To meet such a pleasant fellow so polite,

I gave him an open-door invite.

It didn't turn out grim

but I am sorry if I didn't think about him.

If you need to be mad at someone you can be upset with me,

But he is my guest today and he came here bubbly and charming as you can see.

I think he has something he wants to share with you.

Sometimes a new friend can be a surprising breakthrough.

I miss seeing your pearly white teeth more often, you know they are still in style?

You always live life so focused and driven, you seldom find room to smile.

Can we start over?

My name is Jeffrey and I stopped over

to see Bobbi who I met 2 days ago.

She invited me over to meet her favorite Aunt.

Hi, today is a different Bobbi, so I'm not the one you want.

How do you know what I want? Because many days I don't know.

Maybe I want the Bobbi I met days ago, plus this different Bobbi as a combo?

Or maybe I want to meet the Bobbi

I haven't met yet,

carrying the heavy cargo?

Wow! He's pretty smooth and crafty Baby Girl.

Her Auntie is available, and she makes your toes curl. Lol

Auntie please, you're embarrassing me. You actually got me turning red,

And no need to give him anymore of a big head.

Haha Jeffrey, you are quite clever and cute my friend.

I like the way you decipher and the way you comprehend.

What made you choose to share with me?

Did you share with your girlfriend?

I didn't share with her first which is quite rare,

But you were the first thought that came to my mind when I wanted to share.

To be quite honest with you,

I don't really know why,

But from the very first moment I met you,

I never wanted to say goodbye.

I like that and that puts a smile on my face.

I must admit you keep giving me those and it takes me to a different place.

Smiling takes you to a different place?

Sherlock, I enjoy my life and its pace, it's a focused lifestyle my man and I choose to embrace.

But smiling takes you to a different place?

Why?

Because I'm asking.

Maybe smiling reflects a different place in time.

Maybe when life wasn't all grind, climb, grind and climb.

Being at our best and being on top is what we strive to achieve.

Being sold out for success is what Isaiah believes.

So day-by-day he pushes the envelope working to reach Billionaire status.

His push helps my hurts and insecurities become more callus.

Creating legacy and generational wealth just like the family Hilton,

Who you plan to pass your fortune to, do you want to have children?

Please! Let's not go there,

Right now, it's not about rearing children and being concerned with child care.

So which Bobbi is speaking this debris?

Is this Bobbi number one Bobbi number two or Bobbi number three?

It's called focus Jeffrey!

Do you have the desire to be great and be all that you can be?

Ok, so I'm back to Jeffrey now?

Please don't get it twisted sister, legacy and inheritance is also what I vow.

Jeffrey, Isaiah and my brother Jaden formulated a hydration sports drink called Slake,

They had a 1.2-billion-dollar contract with Frepsi, but Frepsi hesitated and begin to flake.

So, Slake sold out to Smooth-Cola for half of that amount,

This still haunts Isaiah, he feels that he sold their company at a great discount.

At times Isaiah remains preoccupied by the Frepsi snub,

So that helps fuel his drive and obsession, to join the billionaire club.

Sorry to hear that story and sounds like Isaiah is a brilliant guy.

But if that's the answer you are trying to give me, that's not going to fly.

Ms. Pam just said she doesn't get to see those pearly white teeth as often.

Why do you keep that beautiful smile so exiled? It's attractively awesome!

I hear and can empathize with Isaiah's pain,

But Isaiah's pain and Bobbi's pains, certainly aren't the same.

Your Aunt Pam's words were kinda profound,

It appeared as if she knows of something, which may have gone down.

Jeffrey, or may I call you Jeff?

Yes

I don't need a referee making calls about my game of life, so don't be a ref Jeff.

You're quite brilliant also Jeffrey and I'm well aware you keep trying to take me somewhere.

But Mr. Professor Holmes, we're not going there.

So please tell me, what did you come to share?

You're quite funny honey with your determination,

Trying to avoid my question by controlling the conversation.

You'll soon discover I'm a man that's quite alright with unhurriedness and deliberation.

I pride myself in being a good listener and always listening for optimistic inspiration.

So just know moving forward from this day,

I will always be down to hear what you have to say.

That's very sweet Jeff and I understand, but, not today,

But maybe, and that's a slight maybe, I'll convey another day.

You are certainly all good sweetie.

Man, you better stop calling me words

like honey and sweetie,

I may start to like it, and then my sensitivities

may get a little greedy.

Hmm, I think I could handle you throwing a little greed my way.

And so that we are clear, your statement assuredly doesn't scare me away.

But I do think I need to get ready to leave before I need prayer.

What made you pull that out of the air?

The more I look into your scrumptiously beautiful eyes,

I've discovered your eyes don't play fair.

What do you mean?

You know what I mean.

Your eyes aren't fair and your eyes are quite aware,

They keep mesmerizing me and could possibly lure me into your predicted snare.

It's probably safer to just go share with my fiancé and get my emotions out of despair.

Despair?

Yes despair, but it's all good I'm about to leave. How's your little boo Bare?

Wait don't leave, please?

I apologize for starting so abrasive, can you forgive me without me getting on my knees?

No!

Well then Man go! Hahaha

I promise you won't be under any kind of pressure.

I would just like to hear your good news, it would be an honor and a pleasure.

And my little boo Bare is doing well, we walked a few miles today,

And she chilled while I did a little work at this very nice café.

I'm going to be on my way and follow your suggestion, share with my Bae.

But maybe, and that's a slight maybe, I'll convey another day.

Mr. Jeffrey has jokes I see and now he must flee,

Because his friend Bobbi, didn't apologize while down on one knee.

Enjoy the rest of your day my friend, and again, please forgive me.

You need to stop being goofy with your whacky interpretation,

Looks like you got business or romance obligations,

Because your phone has been blowing up during our entire duration,

Could be both, but I asked you to stay meaning all those calls would have been put on hold.

Hmm, that statement is kinda bold and brings forth a smile tenfold.

You would put everything on hold for a few moments with me?

I didn't stutter, I said what it would be.

I said everything, would that really mean everything?

You're a clever one Jeffrey, very savvy with the words you zing.

You make me listen sharply and think keen.

I like the childish but skillful qualities you bring.

I said what I said and meant what I said. You would have had my full attention Mr. Bighead!

Everything would have been put on hold and your information would not have to go untold.

I would have returned to everything after a while but first given Jeffrey a Big Huge Smile!!!

You know you better be careful before you get yourself in trouble.

Boy bye, stop playing with your ego, you would be the one craving that daily double.

Hahaha, good bye Queen

Good bye King

Jeffrey decided he would make another surprise appearance,

He figured after Bobbi's tirade yesterday,

he now has clearance.

Still inclined to see Bobbi and those amazingly mesmerizing eyes,

At the same time he's seriously afraid, because her eyes, held his thoughts,

 from sundown, until sunrise.

Unaware to him, Bobbi is quite perplexed and is wrestling likewise.

Her range of thoughts since meeting him has given her smiles and laughs and cries

She cries because Jeffrey helps her face thoughts of her brother Jaden more than before.

Perhaps she hasn't realized, but deep down inside she's hoping for his knock on the door.

But this time he doesn't knock, he rings the doorbell.

Aunt Pam came to the door energized very spry and looking quite well.

Hello Jeffrey, how are you?

Hello Ms. Pam, I'm well and you look totally anew.

I assumed after yesterday you gave my niece a forever farewell.

First, I'm glad to see you're feeling better and second, perhaps I'm a dumbbell.

You're certainly far from a dumbbell Jeffrey,

maybe something has bitten you.

I'm just Bobbi's Auntie and I certainly wouldn't have much of a clue,

But I've seen a thing or two when something gets ahold of you.

They say it's something going around in the air these days,

Something which can get your mind foggy and leave your head in a daze.

I'll get Bobbi for you

Hello Jeffrey and WOW! Look at you, you look Great! You got a big dinner date?

Naw, going to seal the deal I wanted to share with you.

Oh great I'm all ears and can't wait to hear but I know this time I'm second to your Boo.

That's what you wanted was to be second, right?

Ok smarty pants, no woman prefers being second in hindsight.

I was having a moment and I was a little dismayed because I had many thoughts of you that day.

So maybe I was feeling nervous and scared and confused of feeling a certain kinda way.

Hmm, do I make you feel nervous or scared?

No, I make me feel nervous and scared. Because meeting you caught me ill prepared.

If it's any consolation that makes two of us.

But I see us as just growing a new friendship no deepness to discuss.

Ok great, I'm all ears and can't wait to hear.

So, Mr. Jeffrey don't do like yesterday and decide to disappear.

You forever got jokes,

I can never quite figure out

you taken folk.

Man please, you are taken too, so you can't figure yourself out??

You are correct, I can't figure myself out,

From the moment I met you everything else now has room for doubt.

Hmm, what's that all about?

From the first time we talked not one day has passed when thoughts of you were in drought.

Wow! That makes a woman feel extraordinary.

I'm glad but that wasn't my objective. I'm engaged to a woman that is extraordinary which I plan to marry.

I've read about Ashon on many occasions and she appears to be an amazing woman but she's the lucky one.

To pluck one with your charisma, your mind, handsomely fine and a heart that won't be outdone.

She's the Blessed one, sure she has mass wealth, power and prestige, probably lives life quite carefree.

But of all the men in the world she could see, she was wise enough to fall for my friend Jeffrey.

Wow! You make a man feel extraordinary.

I'm glad but that wasn't my objective. I'm engaged to a man that is extraordinary with whom I plan to marry.

I'm sure he's a great guy but obviously he's the lucky one.

To have such a beautiful woman fighting in his corner, who's there for the long run.

You rich and lucky fellow, Go Isaiah Go!

You're so silly

I need to head out of here because I have a partner I need to accompany.

I have another big meeting for my marketing and advertising company.

I generate leads for car dealerships,

And this year we're forecasting another mile stone to eclipse.

I have a potentially biggest deal ever on the table with Mercedes Benz of Broadway,

And that's what I was quite excited about sharing with you yesterday.

You go in for the kill like a roaring lion!

Your wit, your charm your charisma and your intellect will get them to buy in.

I love the way you process Dear Queen.

And I'm very proud of your progress Dear King!

Well look, I gotta run. Enjoy the rest of your day and have some fun.

I plan to, and my remaining day will include thoughts and a prayer for you.

Now, go get 'em Lion King!!

Show them the skills you bring…

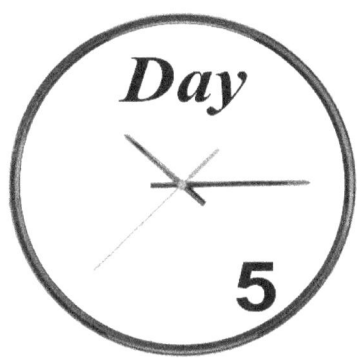

Jeffrey is still quite intrigued,

His thoughts for Bobbi had not fallen off, nor grown fatigued,

But he didn't go by to visit her on this day,

Although he thought about her, he was having suspicions that his feelings were ready to give way.

She still has never given him her phone number so they have no connection outside of his visits.

He thought maybe it's good that he never got those numerical digits.

Jeffrey was in a different state of mind and feeling gloom,

His meeting didn't go as he hoped, so he's in concentration mode licking the wound.

While Bobbi walked Boo Bare she stayed close, looking for Jeffrey's pretty black car.

She was hoping to see him, so she didn't venture off to far.

She has plenty of friends and family all around while Isaiah is away.

So, what was it about Jeffrey, which has captivated her day by day?

Jeffrey no showed today and it left Bobbi feeling a slight heart ache,

Uncertain of these new feelings she went to bed early, just to lay awake.

She has a fiancé whom she loves that's remarkable and rich,

But Jeffrey has captured her imagination but he is still finding his niche.

Bobbi spent a portion of the night of day 5 writing Jeffrey a note,

The note was filled with mixed messages on every line she wrote.

Hoping not to see him anymore because her heart is becoming afloat,

But really wanting to see him because he makes her heart beat a quarter note.

The note she wrote would leave anyone quite confused,

Including her own heart which has opened a door that she's trying to defuse.

Why me? Why now? She pondered to herself,

I love Isaiah and there certainly is no room for anybody else.

Was the note that she wrote to Jeff, really written to self?

Will she be prepared to hand it to Jeff? Or will she leave it sitting on Aunt's bedroom shelf?

Then all of a sudden, the doorbell rang,

A huge smile came upon her and once again, there was a quarter note lyric that her heart sang.

Excited to see Jeffrey but it was a package delivery,

What's happening to me?

Bobbi whispers about this compelling mystery.

Her phone rang with a call from Isaiah and it calmed her down.

Glad to hear his voice as he gave the date when he arrives back in town,

But the quarter note song, was no longer dancing in the background.

As the delivery driver was leaving Jeffrey did arrive,

So, while on the phone with Isaiah she happened to look up, and looked straight into Jeffrey's eyes.

Bobbi's face grew a huge inquisitive smile with a hint of delight surprise,

Then instantly, that quarter note harmony was once again on the rise!

While finishing her conversation with Isaiah her eyes stayed glued to Jeffrey,

As he stood there in his athletic apparel looking alluring and sexy.

Immediately after getting off the phone she gave Jeffrey a huge hug and embrace,

Then she tried to toughen up by putting a mean look on her face.

    Jeffrey! What the heck are you doing here?

  How will that look? Did you think about how this will appear?

I came to see you my dear and right now I don't care about how it appears.

I missed you yesterday so it appears that you've given me something I haven't felt in years.

And what would that be Mr. Jeffrey?

It's not a one-word answer or one-line sentence you see,

When I'm around you something keeps happening to me,

I can't say that I even like it or even say that I agree.

All I know is that I missed you yesterday and that's not blowing smoke.

While trying to sleep last night thoughts of you my mind kept trying to promote,

And during that time, I realized, you make my heart race at a quarter note.

Jeffrey, that is so beautiful and you made my heart flutter so,

Almost every time you left me; I didn't want you to go.

This has been a crazy whirlwind for me because I'm engaged and I'm in love also.

I had no idea that you would flip my world upside down with your simple hello.

I tried to write you a note because I think it's best if we don't see each other anymore.

Bobbi my mind thinks that too, but it's my heart that is hardest to ignore.

But if you say let's say our final good bye, I will respect your wishes forever more.

That is what I want Jeffrey, I can't see you.

You make me feel youthful and alive and anew.

I've enjoyed every second with you and every memory that we've shared.

And something is happening to me Jeffrey, and honestly, I'm scared.

I have a great life waiting for me with a great man waiting on me to say when.

And I will never have to be worried about a roof over my head, ever again.

I understand you beautiful and I respect your words, although they hurt.

There you go again using a heart enticing adjective that's a defense melting flirt.

You're different today, what's going on? Say what you want to say.

Today, is just not my day.

My business deal went astray yesterday,

And now with my gorgeously beautiful friend, I have to walk away.

Life is tricky and you try not to break while you bend,

It's a certain pain when a road with so much promise abruptly ends.

And It's a certain pain your heart feels when it knows it's losing a friend.

Babe I'm so sorry to hear about your business deal and sometimes we don't foresee.

What did you call me?

I called you Jeffrey.

You let the word babe slip out with glee and carefree.

No I didn't Jeffrey.

I disagree Lady B.

Your heart spoke through your lips just now.

And what did my heart say Jeffrey?

Your heart said it's falling for Jeffrey.

Boy stop. Please don't make this any harder, please quit.

Make what harder? Say it...

Ok. I'm falling for you Jeffrey, is that what you wanted me to admit?

But we're both in remarkable situations so those feeling and thoughts just don't fit.

Now I agree, we can't allow such crazy feelings and thoughts to persist.

So, after tomorrow I won't see you again.

Let's make today our last day, it's tough being near you my handsomely attractive friend.

But I wanted to invite you to meet my Grandma Nance.

My Grandmother flies into the states tomorrow from France.

She's coming to LA?

No,

we'll have to take a quick helicopter ride to the East Bay.

Sure, meeting your Grandmother would be great.

Ok, so it's a date.

Excuse me, a date?

Excuse me.

A date, so don't be late.

Excuse me.

Just be ready Queen B.

It's a beautiful sunny day without a cloud on display,

As Bobbi and Jeffrey charted a helicopter ride from LA to the East Bay.

Bobbi and Jeffrey took in the scenic beauty on an exquisite ride,

Both kind of excited and happy but both kind of fearful of what could happen inside.

Both looking vividly succulent and pictorially classy,

Both knew taking this ride together was risky and brassy.

Enthusiastic smiles beaming ear to ear with quarter notes playing,

Was precisely what Ms. Pam, Bobbi's Aunt was conveying.

Bobbi's pearly white teeth has been more and more missing in action,

But something about that Darn Jeffrey, brings Bobbi a different reaction.

Jeffrey, I love the spectacular view from here,

Including the stunning view of the man sitting near.

Flattery will get you in trouble my dear.

Blah blah blah, but you listen here, keep this moment innocent and do not veer.

Ok, but enjoy the moment while you have the moment is my motto.

But I will innocently enjoy the moment and all it's gorgeous beauty also.

Great! And what beauty do you see?

Hmm… Is that a trick question for me?

I see vividly succulent picturesque beauty.

I see the beauty of the trees, the sky, the water and the beauty in your eyes.

But in the beauty of your eyes I see hidden tears, hidden cries.

In the beauty of your eyes, I see some uncertainty, hidden behind your glare.

And a wise woman once told me, "It's something going around in the air."

Hahaha… you know my Aunt Pam says a lot of things, but it doesn't mean they are true.

My air is fresh and clear even though I told you, I'm scared to continue seeing you,

But I'm not scared to meet your Grandmother, and don't dare me to meet your mother.

I'm not dismayed to meet your brother, nor afraid to meet any others.

Bobbi the slight uncertainty I see,

Is because Bobbi's certainty, has wavered since meeting me

Amusing, Jeffrey is back to being Sherlock Holmes, Private Investigator.

And he keeps pushing to be Bobbi's emotional activator.

I was merely speaking on all the beauty I see around me,

During this fabulous ride that will be ending momentarily.

Hey love birds, can you buckle up and get ready for descent?

We hope you enjoyed the flight and hope you feel it was money well spent.

We will return in four hours but please call if your timing gets out of whack,

We've seen time after time where the fun throws the departure time off track.

So, enjoy your time making those memories that you will one day playback.

Wow! He got that all wrong as our beautiful ride came to an end.

I know, why can't two people travel, hang out and just be friends?

That was precisely my thoughts and sentiments too.

Well, I'm excited to meet your Grandmother and I'm glad we flew.

The spectacular ride you just shared with me was a memory for a lifetime.

My first helicopter ride was quite expressive, like a beautiful rhyme.

Glad you enjoyed the ride. You'll meet my cousin Eric he'll be picking us up.

Look for the handsome guy walking around with the German Shepherd pup.

There's Eric! What's up cuz? How are you doing?

Jeffrey! I'm well, how are you? & who's the Beautiful Lady I'm viewing?

She's a friend and her name is Bobbi.

Hello Ms. Bobbi, did my cousin mention that meeting beautiful women is my favorite hobby?

Hi Eric, Jeffrey did tell me a lot about you two.

He also told me the first time he flew in a helicopter was due to you.

Eric, put your tongue back in your mouth!

And take me to see my Nanna over in West Bay south.

Get in my car baby boy but since you turned in your playboy card,

The natural thing now is the changing of the guard.

Although I'm slightly older, you were gifted with the Cool Casanova Style,

And since you're committed now, transfer some Casanova air miles.

Hint hint. But all joking aside Grandma is so excited to see you though.

I don't know why... It seems like she doesn't know the same Jeffrey I know.

Once I drop you off, I have to take my Mom uptown for a few hours.

Ok, can I stop by the floral store to get Auntie and Nanna some Flowers?

Sure, let's stop here Jeff, this lady is a flower wizardry pro.

Great, Bobbi are you waiting out here or would you like to go?

I'll wait here and catch up on some text messages and a little work.

If you get stuck, I'm sure you'll get great help from the clerk.

Hmm, Ms. Bobbi what do you do?

Eric, I wear several hats so I'll start but then tell me about you.

I'm the VP of Marketing for a hydration beverage called Slake.

Wow! I love Slake and I've been watching your brand grow its market stake.

Thanks so much! I'm super excited about the health benefits of our newest flavor, Tart Cherry.

I can't wait to try it. My favorite flavor is your Kiwi-Strawberry.

Just curious, what brings you here to meet my Nanna with my Cousin?

Has he told you he has pretty women in his phone like you, by the dozens?

Well, to be honest I thought he exaggerated about his life that's now long gone.

And he definitely told me about his beautiful fiancé name Ashon.

Eric, are you questioning me in attempts to make Jeffrey look bad?

No, not at all. Merely puzzled, he hasn't brought anyone around Nanna since losing Grandad.

Actually, his fiancé has yet to meet my Mom or Grandma, neither of the two.

Jeff is my cousin and one of my best friends, and he seems to be different with you.

What are you implying Eric? Jeffrey's engaged.

My cousin appears a little different today, almost like, when we were teenage.

Guys, I found the most beautiful flowers!

I hope they bring our Queens visual beauty for many days and countless hours.

Jeffrey they are lovely, I had no doubt you'd find the most fitting flowers to bring out.

I'm glad you think so beautiful. So, what have you two been chatting about?

 That's precisely what we were chatting about.

Eric, I'm not sure how that slipped out.

Yea yea yea, buckle up boy, you're my blood and I know what God has built in,

I remember every place we've been and I'm that loyal friend through thick and thin.

We're here, come in and get comfortable. I'll get Nanna then Mom and I will be heading out.

Wow Aunt Bonnie! I still have my crush on you, without a doubt.

You are so silly Son, it's great to see you, how have you been?

I'm great Auntie. I do have to check my blood pressure now and then.

What's the latest ideas you have up your sleeve, you always have something brewing?

Brilliant poetry writing, my marketing company, plus a few new thoughts I'm pursuing.

Grandson Jeffrey! How are you little tyke?

Grandma I am wonderful. I brought something I think you may like.

Little tyke you know Nanna doesn't need anything. Except seeing you two love birds.

Your fiancés' beauty I can't begin to sum up in words.

You're such a stunning woman and someone's graciously beautiful child.

You're the chosen one out of many, God has finally sent to my Little Tyke for a reconcile.

"Wow! Such an awkward moment." Eric proclaimed.

Yes, Nanna I feel a little awkward and a little ashamed.

This is my friend Bobbi,

The first time I saw her was a week ago at a fundraiser while I was in a lobby.

I met her inside a few hours later at the bar,

Now I feel shyly goofy that I brought her to meet my Golden Star.

Once I became friends with Bobbi, I wanted her to meet the greatest Nanna in the world.

I didn't expect this meeting would make everyone's head swirl.

Nanna you and Bobbi are both in town at the same time for a short stay.

But somehow, I didn't process this meeting would go this way.

Little Tyke, it's quite alright.

Let's not make Ms. Bobbi feel anymore uptight.

How are you my dear child?

I kept watching you, and you stood there the entire time and smiled.

I'm well Ms. Nance. How was your flight from France?

It was quite pleasant my dear, I was flirting, I always keep an eye open for new romance.

Jeffrey told me a lot about you and he never captured all of your beauty in his description.

Also, Ms. Bonnie he said he bought flowers for Queens equal to the most beautiful Egyptians.

Young lady has my nephew told you flattery gets people in trouble in this household?

Hahaha, I believe he did warn of how that could unfold.

I'll make sure I remain more cautious in the future so we don't start any rumors.

Girl, you're bright and pretty, I love your sense of humor.

I must be going now. Jeffrey thank you so much for the flowers.

Just what the Doctor ordered, visual beauty for countless moons and countless hours.

You two have fun with my Mom and please bring out her youthful play,

All she has talked about was that Jeffrey was coming today.

You are welcome Auntie, and please enjoy your day.

Jeffrey, do you remember Nanna taught you riding a bike?

Yes Nanna, you taught me falling down was lifelike.

You also taught me others can't define me even if insults are hurled.

Bobbi, my Papa and my Nanna have traveled all over the world.

They moved to France because the beauty made every day pure romance.

Nanna always said the people and the beauty there left them in a trance.

That's such a wonderful story Ms. Nance,

I've never been there.

France is a delightful place filled with people of compassion and a government that cares.

Nanna, I have a surprise for you.

Child I am 82, Nanna is too old for surprises unless... you brought white chocolate fondue.

Nanna just unwrap it and take a look.

Little Tyke, no you didn't, you created my very own poetry book.

Dedicated to your Papa, my wonderful Husband. My lover & my best friend.

Jeffrey your writings are so wonderful but usually leave me with tears at the end.

This stunning book cover looks so life like.

Is this a Poetic Love story about my life?

Yes Nanna, I want the world to know of you.

The most loving couple I ever knew.

Yours and Papa's life was such a fairy tale come true.

This book will honor your life & share your legacy for the entire world to view.

Jeffrey I'm nervous to gaze because I know your words will jump off the page.

Gently touch the core of my emotions, then get my tears emotionally engaged.

It's something about the way that you write, GOD gave you a gift to write with infectious insight.

Jeffrey, no one in the world can touch me the way that you do.

Nanna, there is no one in this world that inspires me like you.

You gave me the confidence to believe in me.

And now my Little Tyke <u>JEFFREY</u>, will capture hearts worldwide with his lyrical creativity!!

Show the world your brain and your writing genius.

Your words & your rhymes are so cleverly ingenious.

Bobbi this man here is so talented,

He's good at everything.

But he's always to critical of himself and also afraid of what true love would bring.

Nanna please don't embarrass me, I'm happily engaged now.

I've changed so much Nanna, and I'm ready to settle down.

Now ladies please excuse me for a moment, I'm going to say hello to Ms. Baber,

Aunt Bonnie's long-time neighbor.

Dear child I'm so excited about my visit with Jeffrey, do I appear calm?

Ms. Nance, you're so composed and calm, I wouldn't expect a drop of sweat on your palm.

I'm going to have some fruit and tea Bobbi; would you have some cantaloupe and tea with me?

Yes, but only if you let me help you. Can we agree?

Absolutely dear child, because my knees are as old as me.

You volunteering is so sweet. You appear more confident than most young people that I meet.

Thank you for the compliment and thank you for the cantaloupe and the tea.

I'm just another young person trying to navigate through life's rough sea.

Jeffrey's romancing lifestyle lands him in rough seas too.

I'm not sure why, but for some reason, I feel better when I see him with you.

With me, why? Why would you say that?

He doesn't seem anxious, doesn't fret; his mind usually processes eagerly about the girl he hasn't met yet.

Perhaps I shouldn't have met him. He's engaged and I can't reflect any aspersions on that.

Bobbi, I like you very much, you have the mind that will be strong and smart in a clutch.

Ladies like you know the difference when someone needs a soft nudge versus a light touch.

Thanks for your confidence in me but Jeffrey's life is set. Ashon is beautiful, rich, and bright!

Jeffrey's rough seas gives Nanna rough nights, only the right woman, can make his rough seas right.

Dear child a good woman can help a man's vision, by offering him new sight.

So where ever life takes you my dear, I see that your vigor will help any man take flight.

I'm back and Ms. Baber is doing really well. What have you two been chatting about?

I'm glad you're back, I'll ask you both now, when is the last time you conversed with God?

Jeffrey, I want to know that you still know God before I return abroad.

Nanna, never do I slip too far.

Ms. Nance God is my Pilar, my Rockstar, before I knew him, my life was utterly bizarre.

Great to hear! I'm going to play my favorite Spiritual song on this piano, to get your spirits stirred.

Wow! Ms. Bobbi you sing like a songbird.

I was stirred and Ms. Nance you have one of the loveliest voices I've ever heard.

I've put these old hands to work and worked up a thirst,

Now I need me an invigorating cocktail before my arthritis pain gets any worse.

Jeffrey pour us something and let's make a toast.

Will we be toasting Jeffrey wishes for a memorable marriage and happiness to the utmost?

My Dear Child, I'll toast that both of your young life's happiest chapters have just begun.

And I'm also toasting that your voyage home be a pleasant one.

Well Nanna, it looks like our time is just about up on this trip.

My Little Tyke Jeffrey, I have much more to say, how did we let the time slip?

Son, I love you with all my heart!

There's not a day that goes by that I don't ask God why did he allow my Daughter to depart.

Life deals us a hand that is very short,

So, always make sure you follow your heart.

Good bye Nanna, you can't make me cry in front of my friend.

Her heart and love is forever sealed in. And one day, I'll see my Mom again.

Ms. Nance thank you for allowing me to trespass in your beautiful world,

And thank you for the wisdom and inspiration you adorned on me to polish like a pearl.

I only stated the obvious Dear Child.

The first five minutes I watched you,

& you just stood and smiled.

It was refreshing because many haven't

smiled like that in a while.

One day I plan to send this very rare pearled necklace to the pearl with my Grandchild.

No Ms. Nance, I can't. I can tell it's an expensive heirloom, the way the pearls are compiled.

My Dear, I have decided so it's virtually already done.

Jeffrey, you know I'm going to cry a ton no matter what you say. So good bye Son.

As Bobbi and Jeffrey journeyed back to LA,
They watched a lovely evening sunset turn to night glow over

San-Frans East Bay.

They both glazed at the splendor without much to say.

Four eyes fogged with glaze as if they were trapped in a maze.

Their pilot was wondering if their trip together was so fruitless,

It would leave two splendidly attractive young people in a state of muteness.

But quite contrary to what he witnessed,

It was the beginning litness, of a magical moment, that brought the joy and excitement of Christmas.

How come you never told me about your Mother?

What was I to say? My mother is like no other, there will never be another.

What was I to say?

Yes. And you also could have told me your Mom passed away

Does her early death leave you scared to share?

Bobbi I'm not scared, I just stay prepared.

Prepared for what? Prepared your tough image will transcend? Prepared you can walk away from any Lover/Friend?

No, just prepared that I will never ever feel that pain again.

So now is it your turn to play Private Eye to investigate what's on my inside?

No, but you have opened my heart up wide, and learning your story has been a delightful ride.

Since we've been on this ride, you've had plenty of times to tell me your Mom died.

I hurt with you, and a wounded heart can hide that it's afraid to allow new love to arrive.

Well, I have let love in since then. I'm engaged, I just control when love comes in.

So, I'm not afraid but I will Never-Ever be Broken like that again!

Jeffrey, think again my friend, we don't always get to control the love our heart feels.

People abused in relationships often want out but can't turn off the love they feel so deep so real!

And most times with a broken heart only GOD can heal.

We have control over some of what we feel but us having 100% control of the heart, GOD never made that deal.

Please buckle up as we get ready to land,

We hope your flight and travel was wonderful

and hope we enhanced your plans.

You two seem like a delightful and ideal couple.

I hope those words don't get me in trouble.

If I overstepped my bounds, I ask your forgiveness.

And please fly with us again, we would love to

re-earn your business.

On the 8th day Bobbi was quite distant. Her heart and mind stayed resistant.

She spent the day away working, handling business with her business assistant.

Jeffrey stopped by every three hours, very consistent.

Jeffrey still without Bobbi's phone number but decided to stay persistent.

He didn't know what to think of her disappearing act.

He was puzzled and perplexed that she wasn't coming back.

As day 8 came to an end, Jeffrey still trying to comprehend,

He stopped by one final time. But he never saw his friend.

Jeffrey called his best friend Reggie because he was confused on what to do.

Reg can someone fall in love with someone in 1 week? Could that be true?

Jeffrey the answer is yes. But you have a crazy rich and beautiful fiancé, so snap out of this.

I know Bro, but my head is in bliss. Something has happened that I just can't dismiss.

Jeffrey, are you considering ruining the best thing you ever had.

No, I'm considering listening to my heart tell me Bobbi's my best ever comrade.

Jeffrey, I thought you were already in love.

Reg I am in love. And she's the most perfect gift I could receive from above.

Well then you find her and you hold her tight. Lovingly embrace her with all your might.

Never let go, and you cherish her every single day and every single night.

Run to her without any precautions,

Because what you are describing now,

doesn't come around very often.

Jeffrey wondered if Bobbi left town early without saying goodbye.

Why would she do such a thing? Why didn't she even try?

What once had Jeffrey infatuated now has him more entranced.

Something that was once a little seed on the inside, was now more enhanced.

Jeffrey drove to Aunt Pam's early but gathered his thoughts nervously in her driveway.

Hello Jeffrey, how are you today?

I'm well Ms. Pam, is Bobbi here?

Yes, I'll get her, and Son, please help fix her atmosphere.

Bobbi, Jeffrey is at the door.

Bobbi what's wrong? I've never seen you look sad like this before.

You and your magnetism has touched me to my core.

Thank you for the loveliest and most memorable day I've ever known.

Our day together was like the most glamorous gemstone.

I'm glad. So why so sad, and why have you been crying?

Jeffrey, because I can't stop falling for you and I keep trying.

Is that why you were avoiding me?

Yes, I have to because I'm afraid Jeffrey.

Beauty does something to me and so do you.

Well that makes two of us. I'm feeling you too.

Let's walk and talk under this beautiful sunrise.

No more tears, no more cries, just those lovely looking eyes.

Also, grab Boo Bare so she can get some air.

Great, I'll make Auntie aware.

No sooner than Jeffrey and Bobbi closed the door they were nose to nose,

And then they touched lip to lip, where they stayed froze.

He gave her a loving embrace as they gazed eyeball to eyeball while face to face,

Something new had begun to brew, what was once ambiguous & blurry now starts to come into view

A supreme sensation was engulfing them from head to toe.

Leaving them both hypnotized as Nanna's magic continued to flow.

Sweaty palms, wet lips and a froze nose,

Each felt & stood nervously and it showed.

Bobbi I'm so sorry that was out of place of me.

Jeffrey, I'm not as sorry as I should be. That kiss turned my thermostat up a degree.

And WOW, you have magical power in those lips.

My friend, you have made this a most marvelous trip.

I don't know what to say, besides thank you.

You have given me courage and a spirit to face some things that are way past due.

And for that hun, I commend you.

Bobbi, I like when you call me hun. Meeting you has been such a pleasure and a tremendous amount of fun.

Tomorrow morning you head back to New York, will I ever see you again?

I'm not 100% sure my handsomely brilliant friend.

We're both entangled with Great Futures awaiting.

That's the truth Bobbi, with absolutely no debating.

But Bobbi, where will you be 6 months from now?

Jeffrey, are you saying in 6 months you want to see me somewhere somehow?

I'm saying, I had no clue I'd be falling in love with you. Will you marry me?

Yes Jeffrey. I will stay free! And I will be anywhere you want me to be.

Let's take 6 months to make sure we're not infatuated like teenage kids.

Ok, if we are both willing to change the course of our lives dramatically, not just a smidge,

Let's meet precisely 6 months from this day

and time back on San Francisco's

Golden Gate Bridge.

We'll respect it if one of us doesn't make it for whatever reason, our efforts fall flat.

Yes, but enough of that talk, we'll both be there, that's that.

We'd be fools to allow happiness to pass us by.

I love the way you process and every time I'm with you, I never want to say goodbye.

You have proven to be addictive like Nanna's sweet potato pie.

Nice walk, good-bye for now. I'm glad our ambiguity is now filled in.

Adios dear friend.

Adios until we meet again,

I'll ponder many days wondering where will this all end.

I'll ponder too, wondering if our two worlds can blend.

Wondering, why did you stroll into my life?

Wondering, what will my life look like as your wife?

I'll be wondering, why did you touch my heart so differently?

Why did our thoughts & souls connect so effortlessly?

Jeffrey…

Yes Bobbi.

Do you like children?

Bobbi…

I'm all in.

The day you grapple with the sweet taste of wealth that's on your tongue,

The day you question, why start over? We're not young.

The day reality sets in.

To question, does the elation of riches overpower Finding Real Love in a Friend?

Do you allow fear and uncertainty to win?

Or do you explore happiness, that has for so long been yearning within?

Knock knock, Jeffrey once again stands nervous and once again is shocked.

Good morning Jeffrey.

Good morning Pete.

I'll get Bobbi, get comfy and have a seat

Hey there.

Good morning Boo Bare.

How was your night?

I didn't sleep a wink, I tossed and turned until daylight.

Likewise, I woke in the middle of the night sweating with fright.

I'm nervous and I'm scared but it's not because of my 2pm flight.

It's because of you Jeffrey. I have a loving man wanting to change my way of life.

But Mr. Jeffrey, that money joy and life, I would trade, to become your wife.

But Jeffrey, Jeffrey there are these things…

Things that have strings.

Spell it out Bobbi. Say what you need to say,

And then we'll let all the chips fall where they may.

Jeffrey, I don't know if I would put you in harm or danger, my life is not so routine.

Ok Bobbi, just explain what you mean?

Isaiah seems to carry this cloud over himself that he can't seem to uncover.

Deep down inside of me, I feel he still feels indebted to his brother.

He paid his brother back a more than lucrative ROI for investing in Slake.

But whenever Dante shows up, his presence is like a venomous snake.

What does his brother do for a living?

He's retired. He does philanthropy work and does a lot of giving.

Whatever he does outside of that I'm uncertain and unclear,

He did play Professional Basketball overseas for many many years.

He has his own airplane now and he flies to Panama and Alaska on business a great deal.

He appears to be a good businessman but what Dante does, Isaiah has never revealed

What gives you the impression there is this shadow or cloud you see?

Jeffrey it's Dante's eyes, Dante's eyes, they talk to me.

What do you see in Dante's eyes that are so elated?

I see Isaiah's hurts pains cries and revenge, all liberated

What are you trying to say?

I'm not sure what I'm trying to convey.

I'm just trying to explain what Dante's eyes say to me.

Maybe he is someone you should never have to meet.

His eyes say he has witnessed a lot,

His eyes also say, his soul has been bought.

I don't know that you should ever want to cross him, I don't know what he's capable of.

Thanks, but I'm a big boy and sometimes there is a cost for love.

My heart has its own brain, and this is outrageously baffling to me,

I'm engaged and in love with my beautiful Queen to be.

She's funny, she's smart, she's beautiful and oh yea, she's rich!

Talk about winning the love lottery, I would say I hit it.

So how can a heart fall in love when its current love has the heart at its peak?

How can something like this even be possible? We've only known each other for just one week.

Jeffrey I'm also a big girl but please don't play with me, why are you saying this?

I'm happily engaged with my lover my confidant my friend and his amazing French kiss.

What would make you consider allowing your BRAND-NEW LIFE OF WEALTHINESS to go amiss?

Jeffrey think, your brand-new life full of affluence and prestige, would you really be willing to dismiss?

Let's quit while we are ahead. This is all insane,

And to hear your words for her brings a little jealous pain

Bobbi, I didn't ask to be here, my heart just began to commence.

I understand your logic and your logic makes total sense,

One thing I've discovered in life, my mind directs the thoughts it comes across,

Yet when it comes to matters of love in the heart, I can wrestle and toss.

But in the heart's domain, the heart is boss.

When the heart opens the door and allows someone to come in,

That same heart can thrust your mind and its logic into a total tailspin.

Jeffrey this isn't William Shakespeare's Romeo and Juliet,

It's a culture where a few dollars can have your name in the obituary section of a daily Gazette.

But there is also something that I've been dying to admit to you,

I instantly felt brand new with you, so I was afraid because you had a magnetism I never knew.

You make me laugh, you make me smile, you've helped me reminisce

You make me feel excited, you help me reimagine, but I never would have imagined this.

I've barely held your hand, had a couple body yearning hugs and one enchanted kiss,

I'm at such a loss for words how these unexpected magical moments created such love bliss!

What just happened to me over this past week and a half and what happens now?

Do we leave our love here on the steps or do we follow our hearts somehow?

I'm so thankful that meeting you has freed up this joyous butterfly that had been scorned and caged.

Nevertheless, we both have a similar situation, we both love another and we are both engaged.

For the sake of love, we'd walk away from generational abundance in a flash.

If I understand you correctly, for the sake of love, you'd walk away from plentiful cash?

For the sake of love and happiness, you'd be prepared for criticism and backlash?

For the sake of love and happiness and following your heart,

You'd be prepared for your world and love life to restart?

And one more thing Ms. Bobbi, for love and happiness and contentment,

Will you be prepared for family who plans to benefit off you, demonstrate resentment?

Yes Mr. Jeffrey, you make my heart full and you have presented me with a feeling I have never experienced before.

And if your heart has opened up its door, I want nothing more, than to walk through that door.

Do I get your phone number to keep track before we meet at the Golden Gate?

No Babe. That will complicate things more, let's trust God and hope in fate.

Ok Princess, in 6 months during the summer season we have our next date.

I will be there, don't be late... ♥

I won't be late Jeffrey,

I will be there looking for the handsome man

I fell in love with.

And I will share with Isaiah and the world that falling in love so quickly can happen, It's not just a myth.

Bobbi and Jeffrey departed perplexed, cautiously eager, as to what happens next.

Normally two very confident minds, are very unconfident, at this given time.

Changing their world is so complex & they won't be able to call, won't be able to text.

Millions to billions of dollars at stake, is this pure love or that serpent the snake?

That serpent is always looking to destroy and deception of the heart is often his ploy.

Does soul-mates really exist?

Or is soul-mates just an illusion, just a myth?

If given a chance for a true love story, unconditional love would be mandatory.

Love runs thru the veins and hits the Heart. It gives every emotion a new kickstart.

Sensations gain heightened stimulation, while each smile renders teenage flirtation.

Falling In Love, is such a beautiful thing. A majestic beauty that only God can bring.

A natural gift that will grow flow glow, A gift you should hold & cherish & never let go.

Falling in Love, is a ride worth taking, A special journey with memories well worth making.

Every minute of the day, they're all you think of, you feel Tremendously Blessed you met real love.

But then there is the past...

And then there are those scars,

Scars from the past that last...

Ironically, on the same day,

The course of these four lives changed and left two coveted fiancés, quite dismayed.

Both Jeffrey and Bobbi explained to their fiancés with heavy hearts while incredibly afraid.

What they both had fully processed and truly prayed.

They both reached the same conclusion, their love for one another was here to stay.

With much adoration, void of deceit and without a desire to betray,

Cupid's love had touched, and for love, no longer did their surety of wealth, outweigh.

SCENE

The two love birds Bobbi and Jeffrey had now paved their way,

They had painfully cut the many loose strings necessary for them to freely breakaway.

It was a tussle and a fight for Jeffrey, Ashon put up a very lofty fight to keep her man.

She's incredibly in love with him and wants his love for the duration of her lifespan.

Ashon is not accustomed to accepting no for an answer.

She will miss the way Jeffrey's pulsation makes her purr, and his radiant romance to her.

She finally conceded, very disheartened and demoralized.

Their relationship had been so public and so recognized plus very analyzed.

Consequently, Bobbi's path moved forward a bit differently.

Reminders came incidentally, then there's business matters, like a shiny red Bentley.

Isaiah lives devastated and can't understand why she would leave what she helped build.

He's loved her since childhood and has been purposeful to help while her broken heart healed.

As much as Isaiah was understanding and was giving her space,

Dante's mind always seemed to stay in a different place.

Dante appeared to have a great sense of passion for Bobbi to remain with his brother.

He kept pointing out incidental rhetoric so often fruitful conversations got smothered.

Dante would regularly allude to something he fixed, something he repaired.

At times it made Bobbi a little uncomfortable and a little scared.

Finally, Bobbi decided to get more understanding why Isaiah was accepting but not him.

She knows Dante's life style was kinda mysterious, but she would go out on a limb.

Unsurprisingly, speaking with Dante did shed light, but, it actually made everything more grim, more dim.

Dante, I'm sorry I never meant to hurt Jeffrey. I love your brother.

Then why the hell would you leave him for another?

Dante, I don't know what happened but something magical occurred.

In the midst of all my love for Jeff, my heart fluttered like a new bird.

My heart became ensnared, entrapped, engaged and impaired.

I did not search for my heart to become stolen, snatched or snared.

Bobbi you're talking pie in the sky.

That stuff may fly with my baby Brother but with me it doesn't fly.

That's just sex talk, that's what happens when you screw another guy!

WHO ARE YOU TO TELL ME WHAT FLIES!!!

Bobbi gives him a SMACK!!

And she walloped him with a heck of a WHACK!!

Dante you take that back! Don't accuse me of anything!

And you are not my father, nor did I screw or have any fling!

I guess a heart in love can still fall if there's yet an empty hole,

And if the heart meets the right filling to plug that hole, the heart may take control.

Bobbi, you know that is garbage and nonsense.

If he didn't drug you up, then you made your choices fully conscious.

Dante you are correct, every step was my own choice,

And every choice, was listening to my heart's voice.

Bobbi you can't do this, I have invested in you.

I helped you, Jeffrey and Jaden build the life we are due.

I avenged both of our brothers' hurt and murder, so you both owe me endlessly.

Isaiah loves you and you two have that exceptional love chemistry.

The hurt my brother felt when your brother died,

Took my breath away. To see my baby brother's hurt and the way he cried.

Losing you would deal Isaiah another big blow.

So, I'm pleading with you Bobbi, don't walk away, please don't go.

Dante you had Eric killed?

Eric hurt our brother's dream and almost stopped what they were trying to build.

By Eric interfering with Slake, Eric got his own self killed!

I don't believe what I'm hearing you say Dante and you sound quite tickled and thrilled.

What kind of a boyfriend kills his girlfriend's brother?

Dante, it was an accident. And you don't want to understand, Just like my Mother.

Slake was our meal ticket Bobbi and Eric messed with it!!

Dante you have no clue what I've been through, you sound disturbing and wicked!

You will have to answer to God for that.

No, the person who did it will answer to God about Eric's sad and regrettable spat.

Not me my dear.

You will Dante. Because you didn't pull the trigger, you are not in the clear.

You know what I mean, you were behind it.

You were even at Eric's funeral. You're a fraud, a counterfeit and a hypocrite.

And you make me want to puke.

Bobbi I'm working in millions, working for billions and I expected your rebuke.

Just tell your little friend in LA, you can't come out and play.

Send him and his fiancé, Ashon well wishes & tell him LA is where he needs to stay.

This situation is too BIG and too Deep.

It's bigger than lovey-dovey kiddy feelings that can disappear while you sleep.

We are family now and we are all in this together,

The sooner you understand this Bobbi, the better.

My money my influence and my power helped build this brand,

Be smart Bobbi and don't disrupt the grand vision that's been planned.

I don't want to see you or Isaiah hurt,

You're not fully vested yet and I would hate to see your old lifestyle have to revert.

You and Isaiah were right for each other since you were teens.

Now you and Isaiah are fulfilling your brother's dreams.

Dante you sound pathetic and you sound as disgusting as can be.

You may intimidate Isaiah and others, but you are not going to intimidate me.

I understand that you have power and prestige, but you don't get it.

Let me share my heart for a bit.

Dante, I love you and I understand what you tried to fix,

After Jaden's death I became a mental mess, then Eric's death added to that mix.

My life was sinking in quicksand, so your actions added heavy bricks.

Dante, I made a huge mistake and I've paid a heavy price in life for it.

My Mom doesn't care to see me for it and won't forgive me for it.

Dante I exaggerated to Jaden that Eric physically abused me,

I was angry and upset because I saw Eric had a new house key.

I followed Eric one day to see where the key would lead,

He eventually pulled up to a newly built house with all dirt filled with grass seed.

A lady was inside waiting and she embraced him with a hug,

My heart filled with hurt and rage and my mind thought like a thug.

I wasn't falling for any explanation, I knew just what it was.

A new chick in a new house with the man I love.

As the first tear began to flow down her cheek, her emotions began to climb.

Bobbi's words became harder & harder to find. As she began sharing some things for the very first time.

Dante, I was wrong, I was 100% wrong.

The next day I saw Eric, I provoked a fight because I was headstrong.

Eric grabbed me firmly to stop me from hitting him and to just put me in restrain.

All I could think of was my hurt and I wanted him to feel pain.

So, Dante I embellished. I called Jaden and fabricated what transpired.

Jaden immediately came over with a gun loaded endangering and fully wired.

As Eric was trying to explain everything, Jaden suddenly struck him.

They began to tussle and they both became more agitated, the both of them.

As they began to tire, they both now have guns drawn and once again Eric tried to explain.

The house was to be a surprise for me that Eric and my Mom had arranged.

Eric had already asked my Mom if she would allow him to marry me.

He had planned to propose to me with a new ring and a new key.

The lady in the house was the realtor, Eric's cousin,

She is a distant cousin with 3 children and a husband.

Dante, as Eric went to sit his gun down,

A bullet came out the chamber, and immediately Jaden hit the ground!

Eric was traumatized about the incident, but he never pointed blame,

But he was never able to look at me the same.

He knew he had killed my brother and his friend,

Over a surprise for his sweetheart ready for their relationship to ascend.

Now as Bobbi is crying uncontrollably Dante has this look of shock,

A look like wishing he could turn back the clock.

He never heard this version, but now he knows, this love, this passion, and a surprise,

Created an unfortunate situation, where 2 innocent men died.

Dante, Isaiah doesn't even know this entire story frame by frame.

For all these years I've hidden my shame my guilt and my blame.

But my Mother has not and she hasn't been able to forgive me of my insecure stupidity.

Her words to me still continue to come across with much frigidity.

Not only did my Mom lose a son, but she also lost her son to be.

She loved Eric greatly, do you understand you helped destroy my Mom's world with me?

Bobbi the information you are sharing is heart wrenching and I'm sorry if I played a role.

Dante I'm not sharing this to make you feel sorry, merely sharing, I've had this hole.

But, this hole, once meeting Jeffrey, painfully reopened, to begin a process to close.

And not from sex nor parties nor shows.

He doesn't know the pain of my story, but he seemed to already know of this pain.

He unknowingly got me to face my pain to begin finding health from my blame and shame.

My hole began to fill with my tears my fears some courage and some hope.

One day my heart felt medicine, while sitting with this older woman, eating cantaloupe.

Then my heart began to fill with hope and love, she appeared to have a magical potion,

She knew how to reach my soul to caress my hurt and free some emotion.

Many amazing things began happening, she was freeing me from bondage and gunk and grime.

The empty hole in my heart began to feel real recovery for the very first time.

Bobbi, I didn't know these deep things and I appreciate the new insight.

You fly to LA, then run to your new man and you hold him tight.

You tell him I said he'd better fill that hole until life ends,

Or I'll be in LA looking for him with a few gangster friends.

I will tell Isaiah that we spoke and that we have now cleared the air,

And I understand why they both fell in love with you, you're the woman that's rare.

Two days before Bobbi's flight to LA, while Bobbi Dante and Isaiah were having lunch,

A group of guys came into the restaurant agitated and one hit Dante with a punch.

Everything got chaotic during a moment meant for Bobbi's well wishes,

Everything was flying from people to punches to dishes.

They said Dante owed them money and that he still had to pay.

Even though he called off a previous agreement, they said, "it can't be canceled your way."

During the chaos, Bobbi tried to get away, but she got shoved down a flight of stairs.

Where she laid there hurt and paralyzed. She could not get up from there.

Once the guys had left, Isaiah saw Bobbi and called 911 frantically!

His anger and hurt and frustration instantly rose more organically.

By the time the police and ambulance arrived, those guys were long gone.

The police questioned Dante about what had gone on.

Dante claimed he didn't know what brought them out,

Isaiah, for the first time stood up to Dante yelling at him,

> "You know what this shit is about."

Isaiah believed it had something to do with Bobbi and LA.

Isaiah wonders if this had something to do with intimidating Bobbi to stay.

Isaiah had a few more harsh words for his older brother as Dante listened surprised.

Isaiah was in tears as he watched Bobbi being taken out now paralyzed.

She couldn't move her legs as she gazed with tears in her eyes.

As she touches Isaiah's hand she sobs and then cries.

Isaiah, I will always love you, but tomorrow I leave.

To marry my King Jefferey, the King I will forever cleave.

He believes in you Isaiah and he told me you were a Most Brilliant Man!

He respects you greatly, he said your ingenious smarts with Slake, makes him a big fan.

The Last Day Of The 5th Month

Bobbi lays in the hospital delusional, not believing she can't walk,

She keeps summoning the Doctor to come and talk.

She needs to go home to finish packing to fly out tomorrow,

She needs the Doctor to release her so she can go.

The hospital keeps calling Isaiah to talk with her,

What she remembers about what happened is still only a blur.

After making amends with his big Brother,

Isaiah knew next, Bobbi needed her mother.

Since Jaden's death 5 years ago Bobbi and her Mom barely speak.

They used to be very close so Isaiah wondered if getting her there would be bleak.

Isaiah went to see his best friends Mom and tried to stay calm.

"Your daughter needs you, she's paralyzed, and her emotions are a time bomb."

Isaiah was able to convince her to go with him to the hospital,

But for how long, Mom was noncommittal.

"It's up to you Mom, we can stay there long or for just a little."

She wanted to see her baby but was so scared because their relationship is so brittle.

Bobbi, wake up baby, it's your Mom.

Mom!

Hey baby, I've missed you greatly.

Mom, I've needed you

so much lately.

Bobbi believe it or not, I've needed you too.

Mom I've tried talking with you,

but you never allow me to breakthrough.

I know baby and I'm sorry, I'm so sorry.

Mom I'm sorry too,

I spend so many sleepless nights foggy and starry.

Imagining you and Jaden and the great world that we had,

I ruined our world and for that I've been continually sad.

Isaiah watched and listened as Mom and Daughter talked and began to cry hysterically.

They cried together then one by one they cried numerically.

Isaiah felt his role was to be there to support the woman he loves,

While she lays paralyzed and wants to get to the man that she loves.

Baby my stubbornness not allowing forgiveness to enter my heart, tore us apart.

Mom, I was terrified, and I simply wasn't smart right from the start.

I allowed my insecurities to take your son because I embellished abuse,

That moment still haunts me day by day and won't let me loose.

Something recently happened to me Momma,

It may even be a part of what created all this drama.

Momma I fell in love.

Baby, Isaiah is here with us now, what are you speaking of?

Momma I've carried this hole in my heart from that moment on,

I love and respect Isaiah dearly, but my hole wasn't gone.

I was living with an empty hole in my heart,

My brother was gone,

My Mom and I were in the same city,

but our hearts were oceans apart.

Isaiah and Dante brought me into the Slake business and offered me wealth and stability,
I didn't believe that feeling alive and whole again could ever be a real possibility.
I love Isaiah greatly, but I was living with a big hole in my heart.
Because the money, the prestige, the power, covered everything that was dark.
But when I met Jeffrey, he stayed glued and inquisitive to the hole in my heart,
He's been gentle with me Momma; I've been so closed and afraid of how to start.
It was as if he knew there was a need for a real substance to fill my hole,
He didn't know my journey, but he had a pathway to me becoming whole.
God allowed him to set me up with unexpected damage control.
And I met a little old lady, that magically touched and pierced my soul.

Baby, that sounds a little scary

but yet, a little extraordinary.

Who's this woman with the magical touch to heal my Boo's fragmentary?

She's Jeffrey's Grandmother and her name is Ms. Nance.

She was in California visiting from France.

By the time her words her comfort and her charm were done,

And without her telling me, GOD told me,

Jeffrey was my one.

Momma, Jeffrey and I want to get married and I'm flying to California tomorrow.

I must be there Momma. If I'm a no show, Jeffrey won't know.

Jeffrey won't know what?

He won't know I've called off my engagement and closed that door shut.

Bobbi you can't walk baby, and Isaiah has promised to help me take care of you.

Mom, I feel great. I keep trying to tell the doctors and now I'm telling you too.

They said you don't have any pain, but you can't walk baby.

They said if you put in the work, walking again is a maybe.

Bobbi tried moving after her strong passion to appeal,

Then she burst into tears when the realization that her paralyzation was real.

Isaiah stood reflecting on everything that had transpired,

And wishing Bobbi happiness, is what he most desired.

He still wanted to be with her no matter of her condition,

But her being well became Isaiah's #1 mission.

Bobbi oblivious to understanding exactly what had occurred,

She lashed out angrily at her Mom, for letting this happen to her.

The many pinned up years of Mom's abandonment and her pain,

Sent emotions roaring out and Bobbi couldn't refrain.

Mom, I've needed you. I messed up and didn't know how to move forward.

So, insanity is where my life bordered, and you were the medicine that my heart ordered.

You closed me out and I reached out to you until fatigue and exhaust.

Without my Mom and big Brother, I maneuvered through life, totally lost.

Mom, I didn't know how to rebound from my blunder and fray.

I needed to hear you tell me, I would be okay.

Now I can't walk because of someone else's blunder,

If you had been there for me, perhaps my life would have gone differently, I've wondered.

Baby I'm regret and I made a great mistake,

Being away from you and Jaden was heartbreak and a daily heartache.

Can you please find forgiveness in your heart to let me help you, and be your Mom at last?

I love you Baby and something nonsensical happened to me back then.

I vow I will never ever allow us to be separated like that again.

Yes Mom, I love you and I need you.

I'm still a fighter and I'm going to fight & fight until I walk like new.

Great, let's get you on a more comfortable bed sweetheart, this looks like a piece of foam.

I still have your comfy bed made up with all your animals, and I'm excited to have you back home.

The doctors told me the things I need to put in place, to make life comfortable for you.

I will call contractors tomorrow to put in railings and an entrance ramp too.

Only the best for you my Baby Girl, together we'll learn about everything you need.

We're in this together and we're going to put in the work for you to succeed.

But it only needs to be you and I, Mom, it wouldn't be fair for Isaiah to help take care of me.

Because once I'm well, he wouldn't like it once I'm with Jeffrey.

And Jeffrey wouldn't like it if he ever found out Isaiah still took care of me.

This Jeffrey seems like a must see because his name makes you beam with glee.

I know and I may never see him again, with Isaiah and Slake, I had too many open strings.

So, I never gave him my number Mom, I didn't want us chatting trying to force things.

Baby that probably was the smartest thing to do, forcing things usually cause a miscue.

I'm so Saddened and tearful, this happened to you.

The Next Day (was exactly 6 months later)

The big day was a cool and rainy day on the Golden Gate Bridge.

Jeffrey was looking stylish with a light jacket because he was cold just a smidge.

He arrived there early morning to enjoy the air and enjoy the scene,

Excited to look into the eyes of the woman who touched his heart, his beautiful new Queen.

The Golden Gate Bridge is a 1.7-mile walk,

And Jeffrey was prepared to walk it all day, until he and Bobbi would talk.

He knows that seeing her smile, her eyes, and her lips,

Will begin to have his insides doing somersaults with crazy flips.

Early afternoon a tour guide, Heather, notices seeing Jeffrey after the many round trips he'd done.

And wondered if he needed some help or if he was trying to find someone.

Hello sir, are you ok?

Yes, I'm just enjoying this spectacular view of the bay.

OK, we have many different activities also sir, unless walking is the only one you prefer.

Thanks Ms. Heather, I'm just exercising in this rainy weather.

Jeffrey has now begun to check the time about every 5 minutes,

His thoughts began pushing his brain to its limits.

Maybe Bobbi and Isaiah's world  were too intertwined? Maybe she couldn't breakaway?

Maybe wealth and prestige made her align? Maybe Dante intimidated her to stay?

Maybe she just changed her mind? Or maybe her love for him faded away?

Maybe it was all these things combined, or maybe she didn't think today was the day?

Pondering as the day continued to fade, all while Jeffrey was dripping wet,

He continued doing 1.7-mile round-trips as the sun set.

Hello sir, are you ok?

Yes, I'm waiting for someone to pass this way.

OK, if we can be of any help let us know, this walk route will close soon.

Thanks, but for now, I'm going to continue walking and gazing into the moon.

As Jeffrey continued to walk and check the time the evening vanished into darkness,

His embarrassment rose, his fullness of joy from earlier, now contrasts with vacancy and starkness.

Jeffrey usually a sure and cagey fellow,

Is embarrassingly drench and exhibiting confidence of a powder puff marshmallow.

And now pacing back and forth in a small area,

His mind has become over run with slight uncertainty and slight hysteria.

Speculative of his decision leaving Ashon and their wedding planned in Monaco,

For a twinkle in his eye, that's becoming a no show.

But the more he processed and the more he analyzed,

The more he understood he took a chance for a mythical ride; that he had never before realized.

Pure magical romance had alluded him for some reasons deep inside.

He believes this was the first time his heart totally unlocked, since his Mom died.

Taking a chance at an opened and unlocked heart, is worth its weight in gold.

And he would do it all over again, because love, real love, can't be bought, controlled or sold.

Hello sir, are you ok?

Yes, thanks for asking. I know it's closing time so I'll be on my way.

Sir, I hope you saw what you were looking for as you gazed into the moon.

Thanks, and I did. I saw love soar that was once hidden in a cocoon.

I witnessed a love story that played with a beautiful quarter note tune.

And if you ever get a chance to let real love soar, make sure you consume...

every ounce.

When my moon bliss night arrives Sir, I will remember your words, and I will pounce.

When real love comes alive you will feel it, so savor it, then never let it die.

I will remember Sir. Thank you much, and goodbye.

9 Months Later (from the time they met)

Bobbi and Jeffrey live everyday three thousand miles apart.

Yet every day three thousand miles apart, there's a love connection vividly burning in their hearts.

Bobbi remained separated from Isaiah and has returned back into her marketing profession.

A great love for strategy had always been her obsession.

Strengthening her body, her relationship with God and her Mom keeps her going,

Her mind and her spirit are usually upbeat and glowing.

Bobbi at times anxiously awaits the arrival of the mail,

Hoping Jeffrey would search for her and that his search would avail.

But no such luck ever came her way,

Mom would watch her search through mail and not know what to say.

Although Mom had not met Jeffrey, Bobbi would search the mail with so much zeal,

Mom wondered if this Jeffrey fella could help her baby heal.

When Bobbi spoke with her Mom about Jeffrey, Mom would see her spirit set free.

Oftentimes her radiant glow beamed brighter than the brightest Christmas tree!

Bobbi pondered to herself, maybe her and Jeffrey were never meant to be?

Maybe Jeffrey no-showed? Maybe Jeffrey married Ashon Dupree?

Maybe wealth and prestige made him align? Maybe he couldn't breakaway?

Maybe he just changed his mind? Or maybe his love for her faded away?

Maybe it was all these things combined, but why wouldn't he try to find where I stay?

Amazingly the two of them had just about identical thoughts.

And both of them stayed under consistent mental anguish assault.

After Bobbi's no-show Jeffrey didn't know what to expect.

But he lived day-by-day with a smile in his heart, without a regret?

He did not return to his vain life of a playboy,

His focus on his business projects and his book became his inner joy.

His car advertising company began to explode,

And everything he was touching was turning to gold, and business flowed!

He finally secured the deal with Mercedes Benz of Broadway,

He generated many leads with online strategies plus with innovative solar displays.

Simultaneously while his book sales kept breaking previous records.

Happy with all his new success, but he no longer yearned a love life so checkered.

So, at times Jeffrey anxiously awaited the arrival of the mail,

Hoping Bobbi would search for him and that her search would avail.

But no such luck ever came his way, instead it was worse,

Information comes in the mail about him leaving Ashon is usually adverse.

He's become known as the foolishly insane Author,

Willing to leave a foolishly rich heiress at the altar.

If he looked on social media or turned on the news,

He would always see himself posted with millions of views.

It was a tragic end to something so beautiful that was ready to begin.

But the story of Jeffrey and Bobbi wasn't a story being written by Jeffrey's pen.

The story of two love birds who walked away from riches for something deeper within.

A story where in a short amount of time magic slid deep beneath their skin.

The magic bubbled up the same emotions in both birds like identical twins.

This magical magic brought these love birds a vibe neither had quite felt before,

In a very small amount of time, they quickly felt an attraction that couldn't be ignored.

The vibe started off soft and low but began to grow and then began to roar!

A love so powerful it created a connection not easily broken, and a gratitude, to be adored.

Their love was a story that outsiders couldn't understand,

A true story of love about a spiritual bond God created between a woman and a man.

A story of love more valuable than riches and fame. A story of love with an uncontainable flame.

The love story that most lovers long for. A story two lovers would ask, could this only be folklore? Such an exceptional love story that leaves every heart yearning for more...

1 Year After Bobbi and Jeffrey Met

Jeffrey was in New York on business promoting his book and himself.

Marvin's local book store is where Jeffrey's books keep flying off the shelf.

Jeff's other best friend Marvin is a long-time friend and Marvin is Jeff's best bookseller.

He's been Jeff's #1 fan since Jeffrey was a teenage storyteller.

One evening they were going over marketing strategies while dining,

And discussing the different options for Jeffrey's upcoming book signing.

Marvin was sharing different tactics he's been employing to help Jeffrey's continued success.

One strategic strategy was to capture each customer's address.

He mails customers who purchased Jeffrey's book on going information about Jeffrey.

Whether it's book signings, new poetry or his donations to charity.

Marvin's approach is to keep Jeff's name in front of his readers as much as he can.

That will help Jeff's popularity grow, hoping readers will tell friends is Marvin's plan.

Earlier at the bookstore Jeffrey noticed his first original copy wasn't there today.

His first original copy was personalized to Grandma Nance and was only for display.

As soon as Jeff remembered he asked Marvin,

"Where is the original copy?"

Jeff one day the store was very busy, books were everywhere, the store had gotten sloppy.

The original copy got moved off the display, and a customer started reading that copy.

Ok, that's happened millions of times before.

But this time was different, without that copy, the customer wouldn't leave my store.

She said she knew Grandma Nance and she asked why I had her copy of the book?

I told her Grandma Nance was in heaven and she gave me this look!

Tears began flowing down her cheeks and something touched me.

It was a special connection with her and Grandma Nance that I could see.

She said Grandma Nance once saved her life, I didn't know what that meant.

But I could tell whatever it meant, she meant it.

Marvin, there is only one person that knows I made that for Grandma.

Did the person know the book was for Grandma but dedicated to Grandpa?

Yes, she did. She also asked "did the Author marry Ashon Dupree?"

Marvin stop! Don't be playing with me.

What do you mean Jeffrey?

Marvin, can you describe this customer to me?

Yes Jeff, why? Are you thinking there could be a happenstance chance?

Marvin, my once in my life true love Bobbi met Grandma Nance.

And she knew the meanings with the original version.

Jeff, I don't think we are talking about the same person,

This woman was handicapped, and I'm not casting any aspersion.

Marvin you would have her name and address, correct?

Jeff, I'm sorry the store was so busy, and the woman was an emotional wreck.

Ok, this is all weird Marv and I can't make sense of it.

It's all good. But you had me worked up, I must admit.

I'm getting tired now and I think I'm ready to call it a day.

Thank you for dinner, it was wonderful, you should have let me pay.

Get a good night's rest my friend, I'm hoping for a good turnout.

You'll be signing lots of books tomorrow; I have no doubt.

2 Days After The Book Signing (1 day before Jeffrey leaves)

It was a gloomy and stormy day.

Marvin was organizing and putting things away.

Marvin discovered a name and address of the purchaser of Jeffrey's original copy.

But... The only thing was, the name wasn't Bobbi.

It gave an address of someone named Destiny.

Jeffrey was willing to find Destiny, to see if Destiny knew where Bobbi may be.

Jeffrey tracks down the address like a trapper or a scout

Going to a strange address in New York gave him some trepidation plus doubt.

But for a chance at love, is this the right person and the right house?

Then right as he begins to knock, a lady opens the door and starts to walk out.

Jeffrey glances and sees a figure sitting on the couch.

Bobbi not paying attention hears a voice she recognizes with certainty,

And she begins to shake nervously.

She looked up totally shocked and surprised,

The man she had been longing for, suddenly, materialized.

Hello there, can I help you?

Yes, I'm looking for Destiny. She bought a book from the bookstore Revue.

Ok. And who are you?

My name is Jeffrey and I'm searching for Destiny hoping for a breakthrough.

I once met a friend named Bobbi that I hoped maybe Destiny knew.

Oh my! Are you Jeffrey from LA?

Yes Ma'am. I'm in town on business today.

Hi, I'm Ms. Dorothy and I've heard much about you and your Grandmother from France.

I've seen your book also and your writings keep me glued in a trance.

Bobbi said you and your Grandmother once saved her life from a ticking time bomb.

So, I owe you a thank you, before you my Daughter and I lived with an ongoing qualm.

Now, my Daughter and I have a relationship loving, thankful and calm.

So, thank you. And I'm also sorry to learn about your Mom.

Wow! You've learned some of my life story.

My many mistakes in life have caused much more pain than glory.

We've all made mistakes young man, mistakes along with growing older appear to be mandatory.

Jeffrey!! What are you doing here?

Searching for Destiny and hoping you would also appear.

I've searched for you for 6 months now.

I search for you every time I'm in town.

Well, you found me, and how did you do that?

My friend Marvin owns a book store and he and I had a little spat.

The original copy of my book was missing and it was never for sale.

He told me a customer wouldn't leave without it, then he explained in detail.

He said she said she knew Ms. Nance,

And she asked why he had her original copy since she lives in France.

Bobbi I'm heading out but I'll be right back, I just have a quick meeting to attend.

Merry Christmas Jeffrey, it's been a pleasure meeting you, I hope to see you again.

My Daughter speaks highly of you and said you are a very inspirational friend.

Merry Christmas to you Ms. Dorothy and may God Bless until we meet again.

Bobbi, you look exquisitely grand!

Jeffrey, you look handsomely grand also

young man.

It's good to see you, it's been such a long time.

I've been watching your book sales climb.

Congratulations on your success.

Well, I'm still newly making my mark so I'm not impressed yet.

While listening to Marvin tell me about this person, I wondered then,

Could that possibly be Bobbi, my old friend?

As he was talking to be honest, I really had no clue.

Jeffrey, it's good to see you.

You already said that Bobbi.

As Marvin continued, I kept wondering if it could be the Bobbi I met in a lobby.

Out of curiosity, I asked Marvin if he captured a name and address for me to check.

Because he said when he told this customer about My Grandmother, she became an emotional wreck.

The glaring thing was, there was only one friend on earth who was there,

To witness my Grandmother open her book gift and was fully aware.

And I hadn't been nice to that one person; I had an appointment with her and I didn't show.

Why? Why did you no-show? Did your new marriage make you not go?

Now, if someone doesn't keep their appointment, do you think they should apologize?

Yes, I think to apologize is fair and most wise.

The paperwork said Destiny so bumping into you was a big if.

But I gambled to see if Destiny could guide me to the one person that knew of Nana's gift.

That way if I saw Bobbi I could apologize in person when we greet.

Jeffrey, that's very sweet.

I've often wondered about you and how you were.

Did you really? I've said to myself many times, try to find her.

Yes! Really Jeffrey, I swear.

I knew you must have been upset with me that I wasn't there.

Well, Yes! Yes I was, at first I was furious.

Did me not being there make you kind of curious?

First, I was thinking he can't do this to me, who does he think he is?

How long did you wait? Did you wait in the thunderstorm until your hair was in a frizz?

Yes, I waited long. It was sorrowful and terrible alright!

Did the tour guides check on you every few hours until about midnight?

Then what did you do?

Then I got really upset and got pretty drunk that night since you didn't come through.

Bobbi, I thought at the least I should have tried to get you a note of apology.

Maybe you thought of it but you didn't know how to contact me.

Maybe it became your unsuccessful task.

But we said if we ever saw each other again we would ask.

No. No, remember we said if we can make it, we would be there during summer season.

And if one of us didn't show up, it would be for a darn good reason.

Did we say that?

Yes. That is exactly how we finished that chat.

Please, no more questions. I hope.

Isn't this wonderful I've searched for you for 6 months under a microscope,

And now I'm not supposed to ask you why you weren't there.

I have the reputation of the crazy man that left an heiress and took a dare.

Besides your hurt ego and reputation, how have you been?

I thought I was good but seeing you puts my head in a tailspin.

I have unanswered questions in my head, wondering why you withdrew?

And why do you get to ask the questions, but I put in the work to find you?

No wedding ring I see, but I thought…

No, no love knot?

It's freezing outside but my insides are warmed by you and this fire,

And not one inch of your beauty has begun to expire.

Oh, and Merry Christmas, I've carried this for this one day whenever.

Please open it, I can't believe we're spending Christmas together.

What is it darling? OH MY! Her pearl necklace,

Jeffrey it's so strikingly beautiful and speckless.

When Nanna died some thought it would go to another family member,

But she wanted you to have it, do you remember?

Yes, but Jeffrey what about your family members? This is not what I sought.

I knew precisely what you would say, I see we still read each other's thoughts.

And every time I was in New York looking for you, this is exactly what I brought.

Bobbi, Marvin said a beautiful young lady came in his store and she wanted that original book pretty bad.

But when he found her paperwork, it left me hurt and sad.

Because he was explaining Destiny was the name on the paperwork,

And he had confirmed all the paperwork with his file clerk.

So that is why I had no real clue, that I would get a chance to see you.

Marvin said the young lady was... he said she was handica... well I figured he was wrong.

Bobbi Destiny I'm home!

Right then, quarter note musical melodies started playing in both of their hearts and their music filled the room.

Mom was a little taken back and didn't know what to assume.

She wasn't totally sure of the antidote.

After a few moments of silence and pausing, Jeffrey tried to clear his throat.

His face did broadcast that he had a question to ask.

Baby, can you get up?

Jeffrey, I will! I'm working hard and I will build up.

Darling please don't look at me like that!

Why didn't you tell me? You've had plenty of time to tell me during this chat.

What was I to say? I'm scared Jeffrey. What was I to say?

Just like you openly told me your Mom passed away.

What was I to say? That I told Isaiah and Dante, you were who I want?

It was 2 days before our rendezvous and we were at a restaurant.

I was with Isaiah and Dante happy and drinking Chablis,

That damn Dante! Where is he?

How did he hurt you? Tell me how to find him Boo.

It wasn't Dante Jeffrey, I got hurt by some guys he knew.

Jeffrey, Dante encouraged me and told me to run to you.

He released me from his evil web to start our life anew.

While in the hospital I fought to leave because I knew you would be unaware,

And Jeffrey, every fiber within my body, had already told me. You would be there.

I fought every Doctor to leave and follow my heart to arrive at my True Poetic Love Affair.

So, listen babe, if you can inspire people with your pen,

Can you walk side by side with me and inspire me to run again?

Bobbi Destiny, my answer is yes!

And every day we'll work, until every doctor is impressed!

But only under one condition can I agree.

What would that condition be?

Will you still marry me?

2 Years Later

Jeffrey and Bobbi Lamar celebrate milestones,

1-year anniversary of Bobbi walking on her own.

They also celebrate the joy of their 1-year wedding anniversary.

And Bobbi is now heavy with twins, so she and hubby design a baby nursery.

Jeffrey sells over 2 million copies of his book with great fanfare,

During that year, Jeffrey officially becomes a Multi-Millionaire!

And guess what?

The bucks didn't stop there; Jaden had prepared something for his heirs.

He had signed a clause that earned his Mom & Bobbi millions of Slake shares.

Wow darling! Look how far we've come.

Baby, you're my inspiration, paralyzed, but a fighter since day one.

To your bouts of doubt, fear and depression, you never did succumb.

I'll never forget being at Auntie's watching you fearfully park the first day you stopped by.

Mr. Jeffrey, I love you dearly and you turned out to be the most remarkable guy!

I'm so thankful you stopped by, but more thankful, I still catch your eye.

Mrs. Lamar, I love you too,

You're wonderful like Granny's pie, that melts before I chew.

Haha, right on cue. Mr. Funny man you…

About The Author

I spent most of my life in sales and marketing. I became a Sales Coach, Trainer and Speaker with a passion to motivate & inspire people to work towards their Greatness. My goal in training and speaking was to provide information that would render immediate improvement followed by long-term positive results.

I have a zest to help others succeed and live the lives of their dreams. I believe that everyone can dream & reach for their Greatness. My passion is to equip with the tools and confidence to WIN.

I was once a slow reader while in high school. But then I became a Rapper and writing Rhymes was a natural gift. Reading my rhymes my reading comprehension and speed ascended unknowingly. So, I discovered reading something you like in the form of rhyme can help youth who don't like to read. There are millions and I used to be one. I want to give back what changed my life.

One of my two most challenging feats during this lifetime was to write an entire Poetic Love Story Plotline. I took my creative imagination of storytelling of writing five-minute songs and I challenged myself to write a 3-hour read Love Journey. My "True Poetic Love Affair" is a page turning modern-day Romeo & Juliet. The love journey is composed Entirely Poetic in Rhythmic Rhyming fashion. It's delivered along the lines of Lin-Manuel Miranda's smash hit play "Hamilton"

The other challenging feat was securing my first TRADEMARK for my very own writing genre. "Hip Hop Memoirs" Real stories of real people I've interviewed listening for sensational stories of pain or glory. Then after I digest their story for a while, I share their story with the world in a Swingy Poetic Style.

Imagination is a powerful gift that we all received. How does a kid who was a Slow Reader in High School now own a TRADEMARKED writing genre in the world of literature?

IMAGINATION!
Use yours...

My 2nd Trademark is a new character name "BOBO The Champ" whose message travels with me. BOBO stands for Better-Options-Better-Outcomes. BOBO advocates Non-Violence. BOBO teaches "Let's Stay Alive & put fighting Aside.

Be Someone's HERO & Show Them The Good In YOU!!

I've been touring the country and meeting many great people signing my first book "Poetry That Moves You". Learn about my Trademarked Category Hip Hop Memoirs inside Poetry That Moves You.

www.ingramcontent.com/pod-product-compliance
Lightning Source LLC
Chambersburg PA
CBHW020003050426
42450CB00005B/288